THE WORLD MANIFESTO OF FEMINISM

I.A KHOKHAR

Dedicated to all the dreamers, feminist and individuals with an innocent heart who wish to see the world where men and women are equal.

Contents

PREFACE:

I strongly believe in gender equality. Men and women are human beings. They are equal, and have equal rights, specifically political rights which always pave a way for all other rights. Neither man is superior to women nor does man have any right to suppress and oppress women. However, still everywhere I see women are subjugated, denied rights, killed, raped, labeled, molested, paid less, and the list can go on and on. I always asked myself how women became miserable to such an extent that they have internalized the common wisdom: men are entitled to everything and they have the right to deprive them of every right. To find the answer of the question, I researched, looked for answers, and tried to rationalize explanations of all great writers, but it was futile .To my surprise, I found them illogical and unbelievably misleading. No one has given a concrete answer to the questions as to what led to women being subjugated? How did men manipulate women into thinking that she needed to stay within four walls? Why could women break shackles in the 19th century only? However, the same momentum seems to have been lost? What exactly the modern world needs to restructure centuries of propaganda, manipulation and subjugation? The world needs "THE MANIFESTO OF FEMINISM" that can not only answer these questions but can also be a beacon of hope for all the women and Trans people around the world. A manifesto that could give women and all genders a roadmap to act on to achieve equality. I understand this may sound like a complete utopian idea to many who might think that how can a single book of around 50 to 60 pages deconstruct deeply rooted inequality of centuries! Who would have thought that Marx's 68 pages Manifesto could influence and change the world? His manifesto still continues to shape feminists, but "THE WORLD MANIFESTO OF FEMINISM" will also prove that Marx, like all writers, considered women political pariahs. They thought that women were subjugated due to economy, gender, power, language, and patriarchy. Therefore, I am writing this manifesto of Feminism: 1) Answer all above questions 2) Point out reasons for failure of modern feminism 3) Give women and gender entities a roadmap to follow and shape the world of equality which every human being with an innocent heart desires.

THE WORLD MANIFESTO OF FEMINISM:

A shadow of inaction has fallen upon the scenes so lately lighted by the historical feminist victories. Curtain of silence has descended upon feminist movements. Still, feminism has sent ripples across the continents, and no country is immune to the impacts of three feminist waves. Where is the party or opposition that has not been labeled extremist or outright radical just for asking rights? After the second wave, the feminist fervor seems to have been lost as women and other identities are not united in thought and action. Neither they have a common goal in sight nor do they see eye to eye on the question of gender equality. Feminism needs a World Manifesto to represent the collective interest of all genders, and to achieve the ultimate goal of the feminist movement. The manifesto that answers questions: what led to women being subjugated? How did men manipulate women into thinking that she needed to stay within four walls? Why could women break shackles in the 19th century only? However, the fervor seems to have been lost? What exactly the modern world needs to restructure centuries of propaganda, manipulation and subjugation? The Manifesto will not only explain the historical process of creation of gender roles to make sense of the present, but it will also give a definite strategy for the much desired goal of every feminist in the world: gender equality in all spheres of life. It is high time that politico feminists openly face the world, and publish this "World Manifesto" in all languages.

CHAPTER 01

BEGINNING OF THE END: POLITICAL CLASS OF MEN AND POLITICAL PARIAHS

The history of mankind is the history of subjugation of women by the political class of men. Yes! you may have heard it more than thousands of times, but have you ever wondered as to how women ended up being political pariahs?. The political pariah refers to a class or a person who is avoided or not accepted by the political and social class, and who is looked down upon and is isolated from the political domain. Political class of men refers to the historical fact that men came together to form a group of political elites who had control over all political power of the community, and the same could be observed in modern society. Members of the political class often had decision-making authority and shaped public policies, laws, and regulations. The political class of men possessed certain privileges, such as access to resources, and opportunities that came with their positions. They were responsible for representing and serving the interests of only men since women were treated no less than sheep, a commodity to be possessed and traded. Before we delve into the details of the establishment of the political class of men and women as political pariahs, I wish to ask you a question: can you imagine a world in which men and women are equal? In fact, woman walks shoulder to shoulder with man; she is not considered a commodity rather she is an equal being to man. She is not supposed to stay at home. It is not her duty to be meek, submissive, seeker of protection, and an object of sexual desire. A world where she is not looked down upon as a mere tool to be used and discarded, where she can do the job while man took care of household chores as gender roles did not exist, and man did not kill her on the pretext of honor, but cherished her as a warrior and survivor. Perhaps, one may point out that the present modern society is the imagined world. Sorry to disappoint you, even today, women continue to be the victim of oppression, violence, and discrimination which varies from woman to woman, race to race, and nation to nation. However, one thing is common to all women and other identities: they are all subjugated political pariahs that is to say they had never awoken their political consciousness as they were denied the right to engage in politics as a separate class from the very beginning of the civilization. Therefore, the imagined world was a hunting and gathering society in which man and woman were equal. Women not only went on hunting with men but they also contributed to sustenance through gathering and plant cultivation. The economic activity of men and women were vital for survival and success of the community. The most important thing in the hunting gathering society was that women were not political pariahs, but they participated in the decision-making process, group discussion, and communal affairs. Both men and women had equal right to engage in decision-making, express their opinions, and influence the group's future. There is evidence that shows that the hunting and gathering society was an egalitarian society. Archaeological findings of burial sites in hunting and gathering societies are the evidence as the similar burial treatment and grave goods for both men and women are found. This proves that individuals of both genders were accorded a similar level of respect and recognition in death, demonstrating a relatively egalitarian society. Similarly, artifacts and cave paintings of hunting gathering society depicted scenes that confirm the participation of both men and women in activities such as hunting, gathering, and communal rituals. The main evidence came from the mitochondrial DNA of ancient populations that revealed a high degree of genetic diversity; it confirmed men and women had autonomy and opportunity to move and interact with other groups. The beginning of the end of equality came about after the Neolithic Revolution, a pivotal period in human history which had a profound impact on gender dynamics and social structure due to the transition from hunting and gathering to settled farming communities. The effects of Neolithic revolution differed in every culture, but it is generally believed that the shift to an agrarian society brought about changes in gender roles and power dynamics that resulted in gender inequality. It simply made women political pariahs. Let's explore this idea further. The Neolithic Revolution ushered in the era of the transition from hunting and gathering to settled farming communities. It had a profound impact on gender dynamics and social structures. With the advent of agriculture, societies became more stable and settled on crops, but this shift led to the division of labor. This transition led to men doing tasks related to agriculture while women primarily engaged in domestic chores and child-rearing. Patriarchy took deep roots in the society since descent and inheritance were traced through male lineage rather than female lineage. It contributed to marginalization of women in terms of political decision-making power. Women's roles were confined primarily to the domestic sphere, while men assumed positions of authority and leadership within the community. Unfortunately, historical accounts are predominantly replete with achievements and activities of men, often overlooking the contributions of women. This skewed narrative reinforces the fact that women were political pariahs whose existence was nothing short of a useful tool for breeding and child-rearing. The root cause of this drastic shift in roles, responsibilities and basic freedoms was the creation of the political class of men in the Neolithic age. Political class of men first subjugated woman denied her right to politics, constrained her within four walls, tied her feet with the chains of domesticity, defined her roles, and then embarked upon enslaving men. Therefore, two main classes emerged: Political class of men and Subjugated class of women (political pariah). Another subsidiary class of men, which was relegated to status of subjects without rights but still thousands of times better than the status of Political pariahs, sprang up from the main Political class of men. Unfortunately, writers, including Karl Marx, write about these antagonistic classes such as free men and slaves, patrician and plebeian, lord and serf, oppressor and oppressed. Both the classes are essentially men as both stood in constant opposition to one another throughout history thereby bringing about either common ruin or reconstruction of society. In each epoch of history, We find that women are not even mentioned! As mentioned earlier, they were and are political pariahs who were destined to rot at home, away from the public domain while both political classes of men fought for supremacy and domination. If you dare to imagine feelings of every political pariah and close your eyes and feel these lines by putting yourself in their place, perhaps you might understand a little their plight as captive birds[1]:

"want you, yet I know that never

Can I embrace you to my heart's content?

you are that clear and bright sky.

I, in this corner of the cage, am a captive bird.

from behind the cold and dark bars

directing toward you my rueful look of astonishment,

I am thinking that a hand might come

and I might suddenly spread my wings in your direction.

I am thinking that in a moment of neglect

I might fly from this silent prison,

laugh in the eyes of the man who is my jailer

and beside you begin life anew.

I am thinking these things, yet I know

that I can not, dare not leave this prison.

even if the jailer would wish it,

no breath or breeze remains for my flight.

---

[1] The Captive Bird is the poem written by Forough Zarrokhzad. She was born in Tehran on January 5, 1935.

from behind the bars, every bright morning
the look of a child smile in my face;
when I begin a song of joy,
his lips come toward me with a kiss.

O sky, if I want one day
to fly from this silent prison,
what shall I say to the weeping child's eyes:
forget about me, for I am a captive bird?

I am that candle which illumines a ruins
with the burning of her heart.
If I want to choose silent darkness,
I will bring a nest to ruin birds".

It paints the perfect picture of the woman as a political outcast who has been confined at home since ages and still woman has not realized her due place in society. She was not entitled to basic freedom to feel alive as she was considered a precious commodity which needed to be protected at home. The poem also shows gender roles and how the binary division has led to the defined roles. Nonetheless, the poem is an apt description of how the political class of men from the dawn of civilization sidelined women from the public domain and deprived her of political rights. Man was successful in his bid to subjugate women because all men worked together as a political class to define certain roles for women, and then they fought among themselves for power. Politics is at the root of centuries of gender construction and deprivation of women. With this poem I reckon you as a reader might have, if not completely, grasped the idea that women in every epoch of history have been political pariahs. I keep mentioning political pariahs again and again because even in modern society they are political pariahs, for they still have not realized their separate political identity. Even three feminist waves have not been able to undo centuries of propaganda and construction of the idea that men and women are from the same political and social classes since they live on the earth together. I do not blame modern feminists as every writer tried to mansplain history, politics, and economics and portrayed women angels at home. Even writers like Will Durant do not fall behind in this race. He writes in ON Civilization[2], "Civilization came through two things chiefly: the home, which developed those social dispositions that form the psychological cement of society;

---

[2] Will Durant in his book, "HEROES OF HISTORY: A BRIEF HISTORY OF CIVILZATION FROM ANCIENT TIMES TO THE DAWN OF MODERNAGE" resorts to the same argument of patriarchy.

and agriculture, which took man from his wandering life as hunter, herder, and killer, and settled him long enough in one place to let him build homes, schools, churches, colleges, universities, civilization. But it was the woman who gave man agriculture and the home; she domesticated man as she had domesticated the sheep and the pig. Man is woman's last domestic animal, and perhaps he is the last creature that will be civilized by woman. The task has just begun." It is baffling to note that men of such high intellect estimated based on gender roles rather than logical and scientific evidence. In reality, woman was the last animal man manipulated into submission; she gave consent at first, but her innocent nod laid the foundation of what we call today gender roles. These all things are proven by scientific study of evolutionary psychology and biology. The evolutionary perspective on inequality between men and other genders seeks to understand constructed gender roles, behavior, and social dynamics through the lens of evolutionary biology and psychology. It tries to define how evolutionary processes might have shaped the development of human behavior and the differences between males and females. To put it in simple words, women consented to their roles as caretakers of children only during childbirth. However, men as a political class came together to define and impose such roles on women. Therefore, certain gender differences in behavior and traits may have evolved due to the different reproductive strategies and selective pressures faced by males and females throughout human history. Evolutionary processes have influenced the development of psychological and behavioral differences between males and females. However, it does not answer the main question: how did men retain roles of women throughout history? The answer is very simple. Men from the very beginning of human civilization established himself as a political class, and women were relegated to the status of political pariah. They were considered unfit to rule. In some instances of history, if some selected women ruled, they did so on account of their lineage, for which male heir was always preferred. If we talk about the agricultural revolution, writers like Will Durant, claimed that women gave agriculture and home to men, but it was man who domesticated her and kept her away from agriculture and the political class of men treated women as a commodity to be traded. Two main factors further reinforced the political class of men: tilling and war for resources. Both of these things required physical strength, and women for natural reasons could not compete with men. Her spontaneous consent to her role at home cemented psychological and behavioral dispositions. It is relevant that we pay attention to our world now. Take a minute and compare the modern world with middle ages. Don't you think women are now doing jobs that were specifically performed by men since time immemorial? Your answer is yes! I am guessing it as it is a logical answer. However, it was not mental power but physical power that defined criteria for usurpation of power in the Neolithic age. Hence, women had nothing to do except accept the protection of men in those days. I agree with writers like Will Durant, Bertrand Russel, Aristotle, Thomas Hobbes, and so on that women provided men a home and she got protection in return. But, it was done so to establish men as a ruling political class and status of women stooped as low as that of political outcast. Entire history of mankind and every famous political movement and theories confirm that women were treated as political pariahs who had no right to engage in political debates. Even if women did participate in political struggles, their contribution and efforts were denied as if they did not exist. Even the famous political thinkers viewed them unfit for political rights: Aristotle called women inferior sex, departing from the teachings of his mentor Plato who believed in women's ability to rule. Perhaps an example would better describe how political movements and political thinkers treated women no less than apolitical animal, someone who is not interested and involved in politics, since the title of *"Political Animal"* was bestowed upon men who considered women political pariahs. Social contract theories[3],

---

[3] Dr. Vidya Dhar Mahajan explains in detail social contract theories

for instance, sought to explore the nature of political authority and relationship between state and individuals. While these theories led to modern political thought, it is important to note that these theories reflected biases of their time, including the subordination of women. The same is the case with the political thinkers who gave such theories. Thomas Hobbes' social contract theory in his seminal work *"Leviathan"* (1651) emphasized the need for a strong central authority to maintain order and prevent the war of all against all. Interestingly, women in the state of nature were under the protection of men and they were not part of the contract. In turn, men surrendered their rights to the sovereign in exchange for the protection and security which was in line with the way women submitted their all rights to men in exchange for protection and security. His theory did not address gender inequality but rather it consolidated the idea of gender roles in the society. Similarly, John Locke's social contract theory in his work *"Two Treatise of Government "* *proposed* that political authority is to be derived from the consent of the governed. Obviously, he meant the consent of the political class of men. John Locke argued that individuals possessed natural rights to life, liberty, and property.

---

in her book, POLITICAL THEORY 2006. This book gives an opportunity to understand that major political theories do not even mention women as if they are political pariahs.

However, these rights were not for women since they could neither possess property nor had freedom to remain in the public domain. Locke's theory laid the foundation of individual rights, but he did not extend these rights to women. In fact, his writings suggested that women's primary role was within the domestic sphere. Jean Jacques Rousseau's Social Contract theory focused on the idea of the general will and collective sovereignty. Let me ask you a question. Women did not have the right to vote. They could not voice their political opinions. How can they be part of the General Will and collective Sovereignty? Of course, they could not be part of the general will and Rousseau's general will is essentially the will of the political class of men. He did argue for the creation of a civil society in which individuals would willingly submit to the general will of men for the common good. All contractual thinkers believed women had no place in politics, and her main role was to support men at home and bring up children since women were naturally suited for these roles. Fortunately, many feminist writers responded to relegating women to the status of political pariahs, but they were not successful in their efforts. Nonetheless, they raised the issue and highlighted the need to unite for the cause. Mary Wollstonecraft responded to the social contract theories in her seminal work "*A Vindication of the Rights of Woman*". She argued that women needed to be included in the social contract and they should be granted the same rights and opportunities as men. She tried to challenge women's primary role in the private sphere and called for equal access to education, employment, and political participation. It is important to note that women like Mary Wollstonecraft were alone in their struggle. They represented women in general, but women were not united in any political epoch. In the French Revolution, women participated and they played a pivotal role in overthrowing absolutist monarchy. When the time for the rewards for their struggle came, the centuries old " Political Pariahs" hindered inclusion of women in ideals of liberty, equality, and justice. French feminist and activist, Olympe de Gouges, wrote "Rights of Woman and Female Citizen " in response to the "Declaration of the Rights of Man and Citizen" adopted by the National Assembly of France in 1789. She sought to address exclusion of women from the rights granted to men by the revolutionary government. She argued that if men were entitled to certain rights based on their status as citizens, women should also be granted the same rights and considered equal to men. Her document challenged the prevailing patriarchal norms and challenged the authority of the political class of men. Her demands included equality before the law, freedom of speech, rights within marriage, social and welfare support, and political rights. De gouges argued that women should have equal responsibilities as men. She called for equal access to education, public office, and positions of power. The Rights of Woman and Female Citizen was a groundbreaking text that for the first time advocated for the recognition of women as a separate political class. Consequently, her activism and writings led to her arrest and execution during Reign of Terror in 1793. Many examples can be quoted here, but the point is: men established themselves a separate political class and relegated women to the status of political pariahs. They reinforced gender roles by controlling political power throughout history which eventually led to a subsidiary class of subjugated men who also sought to replace the small ruling class of men. However, in the whole process of class antagonism as depicted by Marx and other writers, women were political pariahs. Politics is the main tool man controlled to shape gender roles and domesticated women away from the positions of power. Therefore, to achieve gender equality all genders need to unite under the banner of Politico Feminism which is discussed in detail in the next chapter.

CHAPTER 02

Political Class of Men and Politico Feminists

In what relation do politico feminists stand to the feminists as a whole? In fact, who are politico feminist? Do they have separate interests than other feminist strands? What do politico feminists wish to achieve? Can politico Feminists change the status of political pariahs (marginalized genders) today? Politico feminists do not form a separate identity or movement opposed to other feminists. Politico feminists are those individuals who understand how the political and social class of men subjugated women, turned them into political pariahs, and exploited other genders by means of united action. They know that men predetermined roles for women as they dominated positions of power. Like all other feminists, they wish to achieve gender equality, but they have a clear vision as to how they can achieve this goal. Politico feminists are distinguished from other feminists: 1. In the national struggle of different feminists of different countries, politico feminists not only point out common interests of all genders, but also bring them to the front independent of nationality. 2. In various stages,they always stress that women, including other entities, need to establish themselves as a separate political identity. They are a separate political class and politico feminists represent all other identities as a whole. The Politico Feminists, therefore, are precursors to the 4th Wave of Feminism, and they are practically the most resolute section of feminists who clearly understand what conditions led to their plight and what are the ultimate general results of the feminist movement. The immediate and the main goal of the Politico feminists is the formation of feminists into a separate political class ,overthrow supremacy of the political class of men, and conquest of political power as men did in the earliest period of history. Therefore, politico Feminists' manifesto is to create a separate political class and to proliferate the idea that men and women are equal. Women and other genders are no longer political outcasts; they can set out to achieve what men achieved in centuries. However, before embarking upon the journey as to how Politico Feminism can achieve gender equality, it is crucial to understand the logic and historical evidence for their manifesto. Against this backdrop, let me ask you a question: why were feminists successful in their struggle for universal suffrage in the first wave? Women struggled before the 1st, 2nd and 3rd wave of feminism for their rights, but why did only they succeed in achieving the impossible that their predecessors could only dream of? Let me put it in other words, why has the fervor of activism for rights for all genders died down in the current wave? The answer is shrouded in mystery, and only by discovering the truth can we understand the reasons behind their success. History of struggle for rights fortunately and unfortunately coincided with historical epochs, paving a way for women rights. If those fortunate coincidences had not happened, I am afraid women would have not achieved anything at all, let alone voting rights, right to education, jobs, and etc. As discussed in the previous chapter, men established themselves as a separate ruling class out of which a subsidiary class of men emerged who were far better than political pariahs. These two classes, political elites and the ruled have been in constant struggle for power. It is from the struggle of common men that Women realized that they cannot get their rights unless they act as a class representing the common interests. Men had political rights even in Ancient Greece and Rome as only male citizens, who met certain conditions such as property ownership, were allowed to vote. In the Medieval period, voting rights were limited to male landowners or the members of nobility. The common men had no voting privileges. Even though enlightenment and revolutions brought political changes, the general public still could not hope to gain voting rights. It is in the 19th and 20th century that countries began to widen political participation.

Countries underwent significant reforms, granting rights to an increasing number of men. In Great Britain, "The Representation Act 1867 and 84" extended suffrage to more men by reducing property qualifications. Similarly, in the USA voting rights were limited to white male property owners, but the 15th Amendment to the U.S. constitution granted voting rights to African American men. Other countries followed suit. Hence, women were sidelined as if they did not exist. Feminist writers had been writing for years, but it was not until men had achieved their rights that the efforts for women rights led to a clearly identifiable and self-conscious movement, rather than a series of movements. The first wave of feminism took place in the late nineteenth century emerging out of industrialism and it was inspired by the success of men. The goal of the wave was to do what men did: work as a separate class to open opportunities for women, with a focus on suffrage. The wave started with the Declaration of Seneca Falls In 1848 outlining the movement's main ideology. For the first time in history, Women were uniting in thought and action as Elizbeth Cady Stanton helped organize the world's first women's rights convention at Seneca Falls. Many individuals who were actively involved in the men's suffrage movement sided with women for universal suffrage. This alliance with men amplified not only the voices for the increased visibility of women's struggle, but it also led women to realize the need to act as a separate class. As the men's suffrage movement challenged existing laws and policies that limited voting rights to a minority of the population, women's suffrage movement benefited from the favorable environment which made their case for equal rights more appealing and logical. Since women had awoken from the slumber and acted as a separate class, they adopted methods such as peaceful demonstrations, lobbying, public awareness campaigns, and in some cases civil disobedience. In fact, they drew inspiration from the men's suffrage movement and replicated their tactics and strategies. Thereby, the formation of National Woman Suffrage Association (NWSA), American Woman Suffrage Association, and other such associations were based upon the idea that women were a separate social and political class. Women achieved voting rights all over the world, but it was only possible when they represented themselves as a single political class. The suffrage movement is, therefore, a monumental chapter in the transformation of political pariahs into political agents of change. The tireless efforts of suffragists across continents brought about changes that transformed and challenged norms. Still, how could women just undo centuries of social construction in just a decade or two? It seemed women had awoken their class consciousness, but they restricted themselves to academic writings. Again, events in history seemed to favor the struggle for gender equality as the Second Wave unfolded in the context of Civil Rights Movements and anti-war activism. The growing new left provided women an opportunity to tell the world about their issues. The Motto of the Second Wave was *"PERSONAL IS ALSO POLITICAL"*. It meant all personal problems, like violence and reproductive rights, that women face at home are also political issues. Since laws shape our personal life, Women's much of energy was focused upon passing the Equal Rights Amendment to the constitution. The second Wave gained momentum with the protest against the Miss America Pageant in Atlantic city in 1968 to 1969. Feminists crowned a sheep as Miss America and threw high-heels, makeup, and false eyelashes into trash cans. Class consciousness inspired women to form women-only organizations, such as NOW and New York Redstockings. Such organizations published, "Bitch Manifesto" and "Sisterhood is powerful". The second wave was a combination of neo-Marxism and psycho-analytical theory that associated women subjugation with broader critique of patriarchy, capitalism, and gender roles. We in this *"THE WORLD MANIFESTO OF FEMINISM"* would like to highlight that the Second Wave capitalized on the idea of collectivism, but they diverged from the right course when they started looking at theories which explain effects of women subjugation rather than the causes. Psycho-analytical, liberal, Marxist and other strands of feminism can provide explanations of consequences of women subjugation, but they cannot do anything about the main cause of turning women into Political pariahs that eventually led them to their plight. Nonetheless, the Second Wave did have the element of collectivism which led to its success, like the first wave. While the First Wave was propelled by western white women, the Second Wave drew women of color and developing nations who claimed," Women struggle is a class struggle". They coined terms such as identity politics and sisterhood to demonstrate that despite the differences in race, gender oppression is common to all genders. In this aspect, we can call them nascent Politico Feminists who believed that women due to long subjugation had developed traits that reinforced her gender roles. The Third Wave of feminism began in the mid-90. It was driven by post-modern and post-colonial thinking. Feminists started deconstructing notions of gender, body, sexuality, above all universal womanhood. They readopted lip-sticks, high-heels, makeup and other stuff as they believed it is possible to have brains and beauty. They did not build upon the efforts of the Second wave but rather they redefined feminine beauty and did not consider it as objects of sexist patriarchy. They developed their own methods of mimicry and deprived sexist terms slut and Bitch of their verbal weapons. They went online and established Cybergirls or Netgirls, women-only spaces where they shared their individual struggles because they did not believe in collectivism. The Third wave of feminism has led to the debate on gender and it has led to cross gender boundaries. Therefore, unlike the First and the Second Waves, the Third Wave of feminism refuses to think in terms of "us-them". It is multicultural and refuses to admit a single solution or a theory to explain issues facing every gender around the world. It believes in transversal politics and celebrates differences of ethnicity, class, and sexual orientation. Reality is not conceived in terms of recognized fixed structures and power relations. Therefore, this Manifesto points out that the Third Wave of feminism has derailed from its path as gender inequality still persists, despite the tall claims of the Third Wave. The question is: has the Third Wave failed because the social and economic gains had been only sparkle? The answer is yes! The Second Wave was more successful in many ways than the Third Wave of Feminism, for it considered women a separate political class and represented their common interests. For instance, the Second Wave achieved: more women in positions of power, access to higher education, opportunities of employment, access to pills, general public awareness, feminist literature, organizations of women, and the list can go on and on if we include laws and general critique of gender roles. Hence, the Second Wave was successful, but feminists of the Third Wave could not capitalize on the gains of their predecessors and succumbed to successful campaigns of conservative media and capitalist propaganda. The second wave, however, did not disappear, but it simply retreated into the academic world while the Third Wave Feminists engaged in individual battles for rights. What is astonishing is that it is hard to talk about the aims of the Third Wave because the main characteristic of the wave is rejection of collective objectives and deconstruction of reality. It does not recognize collective movement and does not align with common grievances. Feminists of the Third Wave believe that the genders have achieved parity and society is well on its way to delivering it to them. They claim that they do not need feminism anymore. Unfortunately, women and other genders are still oppressed and are facing discrimination on a daily basis. Me Too movements can give them a momentary relief but it cannot remove the underlying causes of gender inequality. Therefore, the fourth wave is in the offing because mostly young men and women understand that the third wave is hampered by blinders and it is overly optimistic, thereby turning a blind eye to the growing oppression and discrimination against genders. Resurgence of feminism can be witnessed in universities and colleges where men and women are in favor of equality of both genders. Feminism is coming back to public discourse as issues central to earlier waves are gaining national and international attention by mainstream media and politicians. Issues such as sexual abuse, gender-based violence, unequal pay, slut-shamming, and small gains of women in politics and business are being highlighted by the common media persons and international organizations. It is not the purview of intellectuals to talk about such issues, but in the modern world even common men and women are voicing against injustices. The third wave feminists had trouble with the word feminism because the word feels like it represents binary gender and exclusionary in nature, for women only. However, feminism is the broader term that incorporates all genders. The emerging feminists of the fourth wave see that serious problems are caused by the way society is gendered; therefore, they need a strong word to combat those problems. That is what *"THE WORLD MANIFESTO OF FEMINISM"* intends to do: to give them a clear and strong in your face word and strategy to act upon a clarion call for gender equality. This manifesto is going to be the foundation of the fourth wave since the emerging fourth wave feminists are not just reincarnations of the second wave feminists. They go one step beyond them as they speak in terms of intersectionality that deems even if the problem can be the same, but these issues are to be understood in context of marginalization of other genders and groups. The First and Second wave feminists were politico feminists since they achieved their goals as a separate class from men. It is already discussed in the first chapter that men could domesticate women and consolidate their positions of power only because they controlled politics. Political class men worked united in defining roles and responsibilities of women in the private sphere whereas men thrived in the public domain. Patriarchy is an outcome of such politics and economic conditions were shaped by politics rather than the patriarchy or vice versa. Politics is at the heart of women subjugation. Hence, the World Manifesto of Feminism aims to highlight the core cause:" *male supremacy is based upon political power men wielded in the dawn of civilization. Male political supremacy is the oldest and most basic form of domination. All other forms of exploitation and oppression (racism, capitalism, imperialism, patriarchy, etc.) are the extensions of men's political supremacy. Men converted women into political pariahs and few men dominated the rest"*. Political power is the root cause of gender inequality throughout the history of mankind. In every historical epoch, class antagonism was between men as women were considered a commodity, which had neither the right to basic rights nor the ability to participate in politics. Women never realized their political consciousness as a separate class, in turn in every period of history even if some women did try to write and campaign for equal rights they could not succeed. The prominent examples are Mary Wollstonecraft, de Gouges, and others who raised voices for women rights, but their voices fell on deaf ears. Only when women realized that, like men, they need to struggle as a single class representing the common interests, they can achieve what men had achieved right before them. The success of the First and the Seconds wave rests solely upon two factors: Collectivism and political power. Even if men fought amongst themselves for power, they acted as a single class when it came to rights of women. The two factors are not randomly picked, but they have been part of the social construction of gender roles. For example, when women demanded their rights, the main issue was psychological behaviors and social norms which over the years had entrenched in men's mind that women are unfit for politics and public domain. They collectively, consciously or unconsciously, refused to admit women as an equal being on the Earth. The same political power, that had defined women's roles in society, was used to ridicule women's demands for the right to vote. In fact, all rights today enjoyed by all genders are the gift of political power that women got after the long tedious struggle for women's suffrage. Therefore, politico feminism is the answer to the growing gender disparity. Only Politico Feminism can achieve gender equality. This manifesto argues that politico feminism can do what all other strands of feminism have not been able to do. Politico feminism demands a **"Separate electorate"** for women because as long as women cannot form a separate political identity they cannot be equal to men. Separate electorate can be permanent or a transitory phase. It is meant to prepare women for political battles. It is not an end in itself, but it is a means to an end, gender equality. It should be kept in mind that a separate electorate does not mean women need to live aloof from men; it is not a radical approach as some radicals would have us believe. It is just a first phase of preparation for much desired gender equality. Men and women need each other in society. It is by their combined efforts that nations can rise or fall. In the modern world, several reports point out that without the contribution of women economies cannot thrive, and the same is the case with society. Separate electorate is not meant to divide society into us-them, but it is a revolutionary phase. Women must demand separate electorates even if it is for three terms of government. Let's say 12 years If each term is of four years in any country. The basic idea is to raise the political consciousness of women who have been deprived of it for a very long period of history. Politico feminists do not deny the natural duty of mother, but strongly push ahead such laws and practices that allow her to participate in the public domain. Politico feminist's demand for separate electorate is based on the principle that marginalized genders prepare themselves to deconstruct myths and norms that restrict society's way to gender equality in the world, especially in developing nations. Of course, in the beginning it cannot be effected, except by the means of measure in developed nations. In developing nations women are not still ready for such struggle as not only political and economical barriers hamper them but social barriers are conspiring against them. Developed nations are to pave a way for the gender equality in developing nations as they did in feminist waves. However, measures can be different in different countries. In the most advanced countries, the following will be pretty generally applicable measures:

- Formation Politico Feminist Party based on the separate political identity
- Separate electorate for women, including other genders
- Separate seats in assemblies based on the population ratio of women
- Women ensuring Gender equality in legislation
- Women's empowerment and leadership in all areas of society by creating quotas for all genders.

- Enacting policies promoting work-life balance, affordable childcare, flexible working arrangements, and gender equality in promotions at workplace
- Strict implementation of laws against all kinds gender-based violence and ensure access to justice
- Advocate and ensure healthcare and reproductive rights
- Intersectional approach of Politico feminists representatives to make inclusive policies and consider race, class and other factors seriously
- Comprehensive social welfare system to provide adequate support for all genders.

Politico feminists demand a separate electorate to raise the political consciousness of the marginalized class, and to ensure implementation of policies made by politico feminists. Laws are made with fanfare but they are hardly implemented in the advanced as well as developing nations. Therefore, separate electorates are going to shape behavior and mold psychology of the broader section of society in favor of gender equality. Three consecutive terms are more than enough for the revolutionary changes in political outlook of any advanced nation. After three consecutive separate electorates based on separate identity, women will be in position to lead the way for gender equality. The same has happened with the voting rights of women as they were hardly accepted but now it is considered natural for women to vote. The point is that in three consecutive terms women will lay the foundations of gender equality in the modern advanced society. Thus, the first phase is a separate electorate, and the second step is to implement laws and create conducive atmosphere for gender parity. The last step is going back to the previous system of combined political elections in which women are to be given seats according to their population ratio. Politico feminists are not radicals who wish to divide society, but rather they wish to reform society. But, they differ from the liberal feminist who wishes to reform with their apologetic politics which relies on better judgment of men. Politico feminists on other hand take this task to themselves and with at least three consecutive terms of government they will not only represent collective interests but will also shape society that regards women highly capable individuals. To do that, separate electorates are to be shunned after the aim of gender parity is achieved and women are in position to stand shoulder to shoulder with men for their rights. Such society will not look upon women as political pariahs, but political agents of change. As politico feminism involves analysis of power structures, policies and institutions, political power in the hands of women can bring forth change to advance gender equality. Politico feminist demand a separate electorate because it recognizes that achieving gender equality requires challenging and transforming the existing power relations and structures to bring about changes in norms that have been entrenched in our society. Therefore, Politico feminism is not a descriptive approach that analyzes social, political, and economic structures, but it is an approach that seeks transformation of such structures through pursuit of political power. The main goal of politico feminist is to recognize power dynamics, institutions, and policies that perpetuate discrimination, and take actions against such recognized areas for change. The strategy is likely to succeed since women shall be responsible to women electors who voted for them for gender equality. Politico feminists will work to influence legislation, shape public discourse, and involve lobbying, grassroots organizing, coalition-building with male counterparts in assemblies to influence policies. Politico feminist representatives will not turn a blind eye to intersectionality of gender with other forms of oppression, such as race, class, sexuality and ability. However, they clearly understand that these forms of oppression are perpetuated by political power, therefore, they will acknowledge women's experiences shaped by multiple identities and social structures. Keeping in mind such factors, the representatives will seek to address the unique challenges faced by marginalized classes and will advocate policies that address their problems. Separate electorate would ensure that women representing social classes are in positions of power to alleviate grievances of marginalized classes. Politico feminism aims at establishing a single separate political class of women, but their social classes can be different. In fact, politico feminism ensures women's representation and participation in the political process. It strives for representation for each and every class of women residing in the state. Politico feminism's approach will promote women's political leadership and perspectives in political discourses, including women's political campaigns, promotion of all genders' voices in political discourses. Politico feminism is inclusive as it does not outcast other marginalized genders. This Manifesto declares that Politico feminism does not make a separate movement or party, but it represents all feminist strands. In fact, it highlights shortcomings of other feminist theories as to why they have not been able to achieve gender equality. Politico feminism follows the historical path, the very path that men had followed to domesticate women. Politico feminism is, therefore, the foundation of the fourth wave of feminism, and it aims at achieving the ultimate goal of the women rights movements through the united action and separate electorates for women.

CHAPTER 3

Feminist Literature and Politico Feminism

1. Liberal Feminism:

Liberal feminism focuses on achieving gender equality through legal reforms within the existing systems. It contends that men and women are human beings, and they are equal. Biological differences cannot be a reason for the deprivation of women. The key tenets of liberal feminism are individual rights, equal opportunities, and democratic reforms within the system. It advocates for women's legal political rights, but it relies upon the better judgment of men who are in the position of power. Liberal feminist are right to think that the reason for oppression against women lies in their lack of political and civil rights, but they forget that "a master's tool cannot dismantle the master's house". Nonetheless, they fight for gender equality and emphasize the rights of the individual woman through legislation. Liberal feminism advocates for removal of legal and social barriers that restrict women's choices and limit their access to education, employment, and political participation. Liberal feminists work to change discriminatory laws, policies, and practices that lead to gender inequality. Liberal feminism focuses upon showing the importance of women's representation in political , economic, and social spheres. It strives for women's access to positions of power, decision-making bodies, and public offices because men and women are equal to liberal feminists. Thereby, policies must include women and consider their interests. Liberal feminism also advocates for women's access to higher education, and it encourages women to pursue their career and aspirations. To liberal feminists education is an essential tool of empowerment and social progress. Educated women are likely to make better choices and enjoy more autonomy. Liberal feminism rejects gender roles, but it contends that women must have autonomy to whether a woman wishes to pursue a career or chooses to stay at home. Since liberal feminism does not deny biological differences between men and women, and it does not consider these differences justification for inequalities in politics, pay, job opportunities, and in partnerships or marriages, the biggest challenge is not changing such laws and policies, but the main task is to implement such laws and change systems that perpetuate gender disparity. Politico feminism and liberal feminism may seem the same to many, but they are different in many ways. Liberal feminism is individualistic rather than group based while politico feminism focuses upon collectivism and seeks to establish women as a separate political class. Politico feminism demands a separate electorate for women whereas liberal feminism demands political rights within the political system. Politico feminism emphasizes on analyzing power structures, policies, and institutions; it challenges these policies to transform them. For such a change politico feminism makes women master of their own destiny rather than leaving everything on the weight of conscience to men's discretion. If liberal feminism only tends to focus on gender inequality as a result of legal and social barriers, politico feminism takes broader structural analysis and examines how power dynamics, institutions and structures perpetuate such barriers to gender equality. Therefore, politico feminism addresses systematic issues that liberal feminism largely ignores. Liberal feminism typically intends to reform the system to bring about change, influence policy and legislation. On the other hand, politico feminism engages in electoral politics and takes a more explicit approach, seeking transformation of power systems that contribute to gender inequality. It involves more confrontational activism, social movement, and engagement with broader social and economic issues of genders. Above all, politico feminism places a stronger emphasis on intersectionality and recognizes that gender inequality is interconnected with race, class, sexuality, and ability. Therefore, politico feminism wishes to bring representatives of every marginalized classes into power. It seeks to address the unique experiences and challenges faced by marginalized women and advocates for policies that consider and address these intersections. Politico feminism is, therefore, far more effective, often involving more confrontational political activism, representing collective interests of genders.

2. Marxist and Socialist Feminism:

Karl Marx's communist manifesto has been shaping the way people perceive social relations and economic life. Marxist feminists simply integrated Marxist theory with feminist principles and goals. Just like Marx, Marxist and socialist feminists blame capitalism for oppression and economic exploitation. Marxist and socialist feminists analyze how capitalism and patriarchy intersect and reinforce each other to perpetuate a cycle of gender oppression. They argue that capitalistic mode of production is the root cause of gender inequality as women are relegated to subordinate positions at workplace and in society, and men control means of production. Women's unpaid domestic labor, in fact, sustains the capitalistic system since they bring up the new generation of consumers and workers. In simple words, oppression of women is an structural issue rooted in the economic system rather than political or social. Power relations and capitalist mode of production are to be analyzed if gender disparity is to be understood. Marxist feminists argue that gender oppression cannot be addressed without eliminating the capitalistic system that reinforces patriarchy. Capitalist patriarchy is the term that refers to the combination of capitalism and patriarchy. Capitalist patriarchy leads to oppression and gender inequality. Marxist feminists acknowledge intersectionality: race, Class, and sexuality also cause gender oppression. The aim of Marxist feminists is socialist revolution which can dismantle both capitalism and patriarchy. According to Marxists, socialist society would prioritize the needs and well-being of all individuals and would eliminate economic exploitation. A question arises here: why Marxist feminists have not been able to achieve gender equality if they have understood how women are oppressed? The answer is simple: they have oversimplified the historical process into economic determinism. In the earliest period of history as discussed in detail in the first chapter, it was not the economy but politics that shaped social relations. Even patriarchy is an outcome of the political power of men who defined gender roles for public and private life. In African nations there is hardly a capitalist mode of production, but women are oppressed and subjugated. Capitalist patriarchy is not the root cause of gender disparity, but it is politics. If change in the economic base of society leads to revolutionary change in social relations, no such change was witnessed in the economic base in many historical epochs, such as the rise of Islam, reformation, Glorious revolution, and French Revolution. Politico feminism rightly argues that political power is central to change in social relations. It was the political power of men that turned women into political pariahs, and the same political power shaped patriarchy that operates even in those countries where there are no capitalist modes of production. Politico Feminism not only explains the historical path followed by men, but also paves a way for women empowerment and gender equality. Marxist and socialist feminists also ignore the main factors identity, race oppression, and sexuality which intersect with gender oppression. However, politico feminism acknowledges such factors and intends to empower all women without distinction of class, race, and ability. A century ago, for example, women could not even imagine being in positions of power, becoming CEOs of multinational companies, getting education, and doing jobs. Today , even if they are paid less in advanced nations or face glass ceilings, we cannot deny the fact that they enjoy the right to access jobs. Women owe these rights to the collective efforts of women who represented their interests as a single political class and demanded such rights all around the world. Therefore, economic conditions are shaped by political power. Let's take another example, gender oppression and domestic violence was not even a crime before feminists chanted slogans, "personal is also political". The sharp decline in domestic violence is witnessed in European nations, and psychology of the general public is molded to such an extent that in modern European nations domestic violence is a heinous crime. Therefore, political power had shaped patriarchy and the same political power would undo it. Therefore, the same power can bring about gender equality in the world.

3. Radical Feminism:

Radical feminism challenges the root cause of gender inequality and oppression, pervasive patriarchy. It considers patriarchy the main reason for gender disparity between both genders. Radical feminism seeks to transform social, cultural, and political life by eliminating patriarchy. It emerged as a strand of feminism in the second wave of feminism. Patriarchy upholds male dominance and subordination of women. This power difference in a relationship contributes to gender oppression. Radical feminists argue that patriarchy perpetuates and reinforces gender inequalities in every sphere of life. Gender is a social construction as it is imposed upon individuals based upon their biology. People are expected to behave in certain ways if they diverge from their roles they are stigmatized. Gender roles limit autonomy of people and keep women and trans people away from the public domain. Radical feminism also believes in sisterhood and solidarity. Radical feminists highlight the importance of collective action, shared experience and struggles for organized political resistance against patriarchy. Unlike liberal feminists, they wish to dismantle the system rather than seeking changes within the systems. Radical feminism is against objectification of women, and raises voice against sexual assault, domestic violence and sexual exploitations. Radical feminists argue that these forms of violence spring from the patriarchal system. Therefore, Radical feminism considers the connection between race, class, sexuality, capitalism and oppression. It acknowledges intersections of different forms of oppression and pushes for an inclusive approach to social justice. Some radical feminists consider motherhood a hurdle and a tool of oppression while other feminists view motherhood as a privilege of women. Same is the case with pornography. Nonetheless, Radical feminism aims at challenging cultural norms, language, and representations that perpetuate gender disparity. They challenge sexist ideologies and beliefs. Everything is fine as long as you do not ask radical feminists: how would you go about transforming cultural norms and beliefs? The answer may vary from parades or protests to civil disobedience. Unfortunately, such tactics can cause momentary ripples but they do not offer a permanent solution. Politico feminism agrees with radical feminism that patriarchy perpetuates gender inequality. However, patriarchy itself is consolidated by political power. Let me ask you a question. When the political class of men ensured that women stayed at home and played their due roles in the private sphere, what did they do to women who tried to defy them? Yes! You are thinking right, they killed such women. Olympe De Gouges was killed just because she demanded rights of women during the French Revolution. Hypatia, famous and the greatest mathematician and astronomer, overcame the profound sexism of her society. She suffered a violent death at the hands of a mob. The mob stripped her, cut her eyeballs, tore her body into pieces, and dragged her limbs through the town to Cinarion, where they burned them all. Political power has changed the scenario today. If radical feminists can go riot, protest, and engage in civil disobedience, they need to realize that political struggle made it possible. Patriarchy is just a tool and effect of men's usurpation of political power for centuries. Only political power can lead to gender equality. Motherhood is a gift that nature has given to women, but it must never contribute to gender disparity. Politico feminists would make sure that women have all rights because they would no longer be hindered by the political power of men. Separate electorates would ensure transformation of power structures and culture that sustains patriarchy.

4. Psychoanalytical Feminism:

Psychoanalytical feminism is based upon Sigmund Freud and later psychoanalytic thinkers who examine the ways in which sexuality is shaped by social and cultural forces. Psychoanalytical feminism tries to understand how patriarchal structure, upbringing, and unconscious processes influence identities. Psychoanalytical feminism is a theoretical approach to understand gender oppression by analyzing the ways in which desires, drives and fantasies contribute to the construction of gender roles. One of the key concepts of psychoanalytic feminism is gender identity formation. Childhood is shaped and influenced by family dynamics, cultural norms, and societal expectations. Children internalize gender identification based on their gender roles and norms. Oedipus Complex is associated with development of gendered self. Psychoanalytic feminists also analyze the use of language as a powerful tool that shapes gender and sexuality. They explore constructed meanings and assigned values to different genders and sexualities. Psychoanalytic feminists consider any language, a powerful tool that contributes to subordination of women. The concept of penis envy, according to psychoanalytic feminists, proves women are inherently lacking and are inferior. Moreover, psychoanalytical feminism focuses on our unconscious desire and behaviors that are internalized from childhood: a girl or a boy is brought up in a way that gender roles and expectations are internalized by individuals. Psychoanalytic feminism intends to change childhood experiences and wishes to restrict sexist language to bring forth gender equality. However, even if language and childhood experiences are altered, social structure would reinforce behaviors that would perpetuate gender inequality. Only Politico feminism can make sure that children are brought up in an environment where they see their mothers at positions of power and are brought up by financially independent and politically empowered women. Politico feminist would make policies that deconstruct myths surrounding gender roles expectations. For instance, changing children's syllabus in schools can go a long way in shaping children's psychology. Patriarchal norms can be reformed when awareness about social construction of gender roles is proliferated among masses. Politico feminism in fact explains how men had domesticated women during the inception of civilization, and they have been continuing the long held traditions of gender roles. Separate electorate would undo century's worth of propaganda. Politico feminism is an inclusive approach that encompasses every strand of feminism, and it can spearhead the Fourth Wave of Feminism in the modern world.

5. Postmodern Feminism:

Postmodern feminism emerged in the late 20th century and it draws from postmodern philosophy and critical theory. Postmodern feminism questions grand narrative, fixed identities, gender roles, knowledge, power as they are socially constructed. It challenges traditional approaches to gender equality. Gender disparity is shaped by language, discourse, and cultural norms. In turn, postmodern feminism criticizes the binary categories such as female male, masculine or feminine, and heterosexual or homosexual. It simply rejects that these categories are fixed, and emphasizes that these are social constructions. Postmodern feminists define the role of language, discourses and cultural representations in constructing gender roles and power relations. Language is gendered and therefore it shapes gender identity. Postmodern feminism also examines the relationship between power and knowledge because knowledge cannot be neutral as it is influenced by power structures. Hence, postmodern feminism focuses upon subjectivity of knowledge, identity and power. The most important aspect of postmodern feminism is that it advocates for political activism for social change and transformation of oppressive structures. It in fact encourages activism that is aware of power dynamics and seeks to disrupt dominant discourse. Politico feminism encompasses almost all concepts of postmodern feminism as it aims at disrupting dominant discourses by giving women political power. Power relations cannot be changed until the power is transferred to women. Political power is only possible when women are given a separate electorate to deconstruct sexist language, gender roles, knowledge and identity. However, Politico feminism believes in collectivism, unlike the third wave which takes an individual approach. Only by becoming a single political class can women create new truths and power relations that ensure gender parity. Social classes can be different based on race, ethnicity, class, and sex, but they all must be represented as a single political class so as to represent the collective interests keeping in mind intersections. Emancipatory politics that postmodern feminism emphasizes is only possible through Politico feminism. Hence, Politico feminism is a beacon of hope for postmodern feminists around the world.

6. Postcolonial feminism:

Postcolonial feminism analyzes intersections of gender, race, class, and colonialism. As mainstream gender theories failed to address experiences and struggles of women in postcolonial countries, postcolonial feminism emerged as a response which considers the impact of colonialism on women. Postcolonial feminism recognized the profound impact of postcolonial and neo colonial practices on gender equality. For example, intersections of gender with race, class, ethnicity, and colonial legacy shaped the status of women in colonized countries as colonial powers imposed their ideologies, norms, and systems of oppression in the colonized societies. Postcolonial feminism seeks to dismantle colonial legacy and calls for decolonization of institutions and discourses that put women in subordinate positions. Postcolonial feminists engage in activism to empower marginalized classes and to challenge racial inequalities. Postcolonial feminists became the voice of women from postcolonial contexts who were ignored by mainstream feminism. Postcolonial feminism acknowledges the diversity of women's experiences and strives for gender parity. Postcolonial feminism emphasizes transnational solidarity and activism. It believes in interconnectedness of struggle against gender oppression, racial injustice and economic exploitation. Politico feminism also believes in the interconnectedness of the struggle for gender equality. Politico feminism intends to establish a transnational alliance of women in which women from post colonized countries work in tandem with mainstream gender equality measures.

However, in colonized countries women face not only legal barriers but also social barriers. Therefore, in the first stage separate electorates would be spearheaded by advanced nations and they will pave a way for the developing countries. Politico feminists will use international organizations to reach to women in colonized countries and women in the colonized countries can initiate their own struggle for separate electorates in their own countries. Since politico feminism recognizes diversity of women's experiences and acknowledges intersections, it is an inclusive approach that encourages representatives of every class of women to highlight their issues through their political representatives. Politico feminism doesn't rely upon the mercy of men, but enables genders to take hold of their destiny and usher in the new era of gender equality around the world. Politico feminism is the way forward for the international movement for gender equality in the world.

7. Cultural Feminism:

Cultural feminism celebrates and values cultural and biological differences from men. It refers to the idea that women are innately different and possess evolved essence which distinguishes them from men. Culture at large has historically qualified women's essence as a weakness, but women's essence gives women a societal advantage over men. Cultural feminists argue that women possess unique qualities and attributes, and perspectives that need to be valued in order to create gender parity. Cultural feminism uses essentialist arguments that assert women's inherent qualities and strength are different from men. These different attributes in fact contribute to women's unique experiences and capabilities. Motherhood and care giving are one of such capabilities, and cultural feminism places strong emphasis on roles and qualities of women, such as empathy, compassion, and communal harmony. Cultural feminists strive for female solidarity and community building so that women could come together to support one another and create a sense of sisterhood. Critics point out the essentialist nature of arguments and outright denial of women's diverse experiences, and they highlight cultural feminists' disregard of intersections of race and other forms of social inequalities. Nonetheless, Politico feminism recognizes women's biological differences and values women's attributes, but these differences must not be a reason for women subjugation and their fixed gender roles. Politico feminism struggles for women rights in all circumstances. Separate electorates is not only a demand for gaining political power, but it is ,in reality, a means of translating every will into policies, laws, strategies and practices to incorporate every voice and address grievances of all sections of society. Indeed, women are blessed with different biology, but it does not mean that it should be exploited as a reason for gender inequality. Politico feminism strives for a society where women with their natural attributes and qualities are confident, empowered, and successful like men.

8. Ecofeminism:

Ecofeminism argues that oppression and exploitation of women and the environment are interconnected. Ecofeminists align the historical and present-day oppression of men and environment; they argue that patriarchal societies have dominated women and the environment as women's experiences of oppression often overlapped with environmental degradation. Ecofeminism recognizes intersections of gender, race, and class. Women are disproportionately affected by environmental destruction and climate change. Ecofeminists also challenge the dualist thinking separating environment and women. They argue that patriarchal worldview separates women from nature as they separate women from men. Men have monopolized means of production and they prioritize profit over the well-being of mankind and environment. Ecofeminism suggests social justice, sustainability over domination and unbridled profit-making. Hence, ecofeminism emphasizes the importance of feminine perspectives, and practices in addressing environmental issues because women have historically played roles in nurturing and sustaining communities. Ecofeminism, therefore, seeks recognition and inclusion of women's knowledge and voices for environmental decision-making. Ecofeminists call to action and encourage protests to address environmental degradation. However, such protests and activism can hardly influence policies of rulers until and unless women are in positions of power. Politico feminism with its demand for a separate electorate will make sure that women address ecofeminists' grievances and concerns. It is the truth that men have monopolized economic forces because they controlled political power in every epoch of history. Even today, women continue to be affected by environmental degradation more than men. As they give birth and are vulnerable to malnutrition, politico feminism is the natural course for women emancipation and protection of women. As far as the capitalist system is concerned, the capitalist system historically calibrated its standing when a new political situation emerges. In turn, political power in the hands of women would spearhead change in the economic system, incorporating policies and practices that usher in the new era of gender equality.

Politico Feminism is inclusive in nature, thereby it also addresses queer feminism and intersectional feminism. As long as an individual of any sexuality or identity subscribes to the ideals of politico feminism, he or she is a politico feminist. Such a person can represent issues of their communities. Politico feminism is the fountain of political power that represents all feminists and feminism strands and it strives to achieve the ultimate goal of feminist movements. Politico feminists do not form a separate party or ideology; rather it is an ultimate movement incorporating core principles, values, dreams, and aspirations, of every feminist. Oh! Women and subjugated genders of the world unite in thought and action: You have nothing to lose except for centuries of subjugation and chains of gender role expectations.

CHAPTER: 04

POLITICO FEMINISTS' CONFESSIONS OF FAITH AND PRINCIPLES:

Nothing can explain in detail politico feminists' confessions of faith and principles than the dialogue in form of an interview:

Question1: Who is Politico Feminist?

Answer: Politico feminist is an individual who believes in collectivism, wishes political power for marginalized genders, and demands a separate electorate for them.

Question 2: What is the aim of politico feminists?

Answer: To secure a separate electorate for women so that they could pave a way for gender equality in society.

Question 3: How do you wish to achieve this aim?

Answer: By eliminating political dominance of men and enabling women to hold positions of power.

Question 4: On what do you base your demand for a separate electorate for women?

Answer: Firstly, on the fact that women were turned into political pariahs by using political power resulting from established ruling political class of men. Secondly, on the formation of gender roles and their reinforcement through political power as there exists an irrefutable historical fact that even women themselves felt protected at home. Lastly, the fact that political power brought women into public domain and the same political power can create gender parity in the modern world.

Question 5: What are the principles of such political power?
Answer: Principles are derived from the historical process that at every epoch in human history women were denied the right to participate in politics and, even if they did participate, their contribution was denied and fruits of struggle were restricted to men only. Therefore, the first principle is political participation. The second principle of such political power is inclusiveness. Men domesticated women on account of her biological differences, but such exploitation would only create a new subjugated class. In turn, the second principle of political power that we wish to achieve is inclusiveness; all genders who subscribe to political philosophy of politico feminism can be members of politico feminist party. The last principle is collaboration with all intersections and even men.

Question 6: How do You wish to prepare a way for the political power of women and subjugated genders?

Answer: By enlightening and uniting all feminists under the banner of political feminism as Political feminism is the collective representative of aspirations of all genders and all strands of feminism.

Question 7: It is still confusing. Are liberal feminists and politico feminist not the same?

Answer: No! They are not the same. Liberal feminists strive to bring reforms within the system whereas politico feminists strive to be agents of change. Liberal feminists rely on the men's discretion, but politico feminists want a separate electorate and wish to convert their demands into policies. Liberal feminism is an individual approach while politico feminism is a collective approach to the question of gender equality. Take an example of a policy demanding rights of women in the industrial sector. Liberal feminists would highlight shortcomings and suggest reforms. However, politico feminists would formulate the policy themselves and they would, if needed, change some sections of policies based on their personal and collective aspirations.

Question 8: Then there have not always been politico feminists?

Answer: No. There have always been feminists who demanded equal rights for women and men. But, there have not always been politico feminists who demanded a separate electorate based on genders and believed in collectivism for achieving equal rights for men and women. Mary Wollstonecraft, Olympe De gouges, and other writers and activists were feminists but they were not politico feminists.

Question 9: When did politico feminism start?

Answer: Politico feminism derives its demands from the historical path that men followed to subjugate and domesticate women. So, Politico feminism started from the day when men controlled political power and set out to define gender roles. Politico feminism intends to bring back equality that men and women enjoyed in hunting and gathering society in which man and woman were equal. women not only went on hunting with men but they also contributed to sustenance through gathering and plant cultivation. The economic activity of men and women were vital for survival and success of the community. The most important thing in the hunting gathering society was that women were not political pariahs, but they participated in the decision-making process, group discussion, and communal affairs. Both men and women had opportunities to participate in decision-making, express their opinions, and influence the group's future. The beginning of the end of equality came about after the Neolithic Revolution. It was a pivotal period in human history which had a profound impact on gender dynamics and social structure due to the transition from hunting and gathering to settled farming communities. The effects of Neolithic revolution differed in every culture, but it is generally believed that the shift to an agrarian society brought about changes in gender roles and power dynamics that resulted in gender inequality. It simply made women political pariahs. With the advent of agriculture, societies became more stable and settled on crops, but this shift led to the division of labor. This transition led to men doing tasks related to agriculture while women primarily engaged in domestic chores and child-rearing. Patriarchy took deep roots in the society since descent and inheritance were traced through male lineage rather than female lineage. It contributed to marginalization of women in terms of political decision-making power. Women's roles were confined primarily to the domestic sphere, while men assumed positions of authority and leadership within the community. The root cause of this drastic shift in roles, responsibilities and basic freedoms was the creation of the political class of men in the Neolithic age. Political class of men first subjugated women, denied her right to politics, constrained her within four walls, tied her feet with the chains of domesticity, defined her roles, and then embarked upon enslaving men. Thus, the starting point of politico feminism is the 19th and early 20th century, but its roots are derived from the history. Men had maintained political power until the 19th and 20th century, but women started demanding political rights as a separate class in the 19th century and gained right to vote. Hence, women can rise to power today only when they would demand a separate electorate to achieve gender parity in society.

Question 10: How will politico feminists rise to political power?

Answer: The first step, of course, is to form a politico feminist party in every country around the world. The Politico feminist party would lobby, protest, initiate a campaign, and engage in civil disobedience for a separate electorate. Once the party is allowed a separate electorate, membership needs to be opened for all genders who are committed to politico feminists ideology of collectivism and separate political identity. Seats in national assemblies and provincial assemblies need to be distributed according to the women population; this would ensure that the maximum number of women and other genders are given the right to hold a political office. The road may seem straightforward, but the struggle may take years or even sacrifices of women and other genders. However, it is the only way to gender equality in the present world because politico feminism is committed to dismantle power structures and reform them so as to create gender parity in power relations.

Question 11: Then You do not believe that a separate electorate has been possible at any time?

Answer: No. The separate electorate has only arisen after women achieved the right to vote which made it possible for women to struggle for her economic and social rights. When women realized that they had to unite as men did when they demanded their political rights. They even applied men's strategies and practices for the right to vote. Turn pages of history, you would not find any historical period in which women represented collective interests and came together to demand their rights. You will find only some women like Hypatia, Mary wollstonecraft, Olympe de gouges, and countless other women who demanded rights, but they could not achieve anything other than the sympathy of some educated men. However, something unprecedented happened in history when women collectively strived for their rights and political rights emboldened her to demand rights in private life. The whole story of how men controlled political power in the beginning of civilization in the Neolithic revolution points out that in the subsequent history women had given their consent to their subordinate position. In fact they had accepted themselves as political pariahs. Therefore, a separate electorate is possible now as the fourth wave of feminism is in the offing and success of third wave pales against the second and the first wave because third wave believes in individual approach to the problem of gender inequality. Time has come for women to demand a separate electorate now.

Question 12: Let's go back to the previous question. As you wish to create a separate electorate for women by enlightening and uniting feminists, then you reject revolution?

Answer: Demanding a separate electorate is a revolution in itself. It is something that has never been demanded nor has it ever been in the wild imagination of feminists. We are aware that change of such magnitude would not happen without resistance, but we believe in political struggle. Sooner or later separate electorates are bound to happen. Therefore, in this sense we endorse revolution that will transform how power relations and social structure operate.

Question 13: How will the prime minister or president be selected if separate electorates for women are achieved?

Answer: We do not wish to divide society in us-them, but rather just wish to achieve gender parity. Let's suppose if we are talking about presidential elections, two candidates can be selected by mutual consultation. Even if both of them are males, they would have to keep in mind that half of the population's votes and seats in the Senate are contingent upon their efforts for gender equality. See we do not wish to destroy the political systems. We only want to make the political system more inclusive.

Question 14: Do you intend to replace the existing social order?

Answer: We have no such intention, but we do wish to reform it. Patriarchy is interconnected with the political power of men. Once political power is evenly distributed, the coercive power that reinforced patriarchy for centuries would also crumble, thereby leading to a more balanced society. Take an example of modern European society. A century ago, patriarchy was deep rooted in society. It all changed when women struggled together as a class to initiate campaigns, protest, and participate in politics. Psychology of the next generation is molded in favor of gender parity. Politico feminism is committed to continue this path and lead to the ultimate goal of an egalitarian society based on gender equality.

Question 15: What will be your first measure once you have established a separate electorate for women?
Answer: Guaranteeing rights of all genders.

Question 16: How will you do this?
Answer: 1. By making sure that all genders are given rights through legislation, policies, and practices and such measures would be strictly implemented.

2. By selecting representatives of each subjugated genders in order to give voice to every intersection in decision-making processes.

3. By giving equal economic opportunities and making sure that gender equality is pervasive at the workplace. By assigning separate quotas for women and genders to ensure their contribution in the economy.

4. By continuously engaging in alliances and dialogues with all stakeholders to make sure no class feels like a political pariah.

Question 17: You keep mentioning political pariahs. What are they?

Answer: Political pariahs are individuals who are not accepted in the political process. Although politics shapes their life and influences every phase of their existence, still they are political outcasts whose opinions do not matter. For a very long period, women were political pariahs. In fact, they are still political pariahs in many developing nations because on paper they have all the rights, but in reality they have no right to participate in politics.

Question 18: How do you see the effects of separate electorates on the family system?

Answer: We are absolutely not against the family system. We cherish the natural role of motherhood. It is something that men can never have. However, we are against the imposed patriarchal values that women have no place in public domain and they are sweet angels who should remain at home. Politico feminism agrees with cultural feminism in appreciating natural attributes of women, but it also values radical feminism's perspective that patriarchal norms need to be reformed or eliminated. Political power of women will kill two birds with a single stone: celebrate nurturing attributes of women and challenge patriarchal norms. The Second Wave's "Personal is also political" is the way forward for family issues like domestic violence.

Question 19: Politico Feminism is against the capitalist system?

Answer: Politico feminism is against how forces of production are distributed and how political power has been misused to exploit the environment and natural resources. Politico feminism is not against any economic system as long as the underlying principles of the system employ gender parity. Capitalism always modifies itself according to changing circumstances as it did during the peak of the cold war. Capitalist countries initiated socialist policies such as health cards and social programs. Therefore, once women are in power, capitalism would change its course. If it does not change at all, remember women are no longer helpless political pariahs. They can, if needed, dismantle the whole system of capitalism.

Question 20: Politico feminism is all about women rights?

Answer: No. It is not only about women rights. It is about the rights of all subjugated genders. When we demand separate electorates we do not only demand it for women but all other identities as well. However, they all need to be part of the Politico feminist party that seeks to achieve gender equality.

Question 21: Why do you then emphasize women in your Manifesto?

Answer: It is a matter of statistics and numbers. Women make up half of the population of the world, and when we use the word women, we are including and representing all genders.

Question 22: What is the difference between a politician and Politico feminist?

Answer: Both engage in politics, but the goals are different. A woman politician may or may not emphasize on policies for gender equality, but a Politico feminist politician will not only help formulate gender policies, but will also represent collective interests of the group.

Question 23: Is politico feminism similar to postmodern feminism?

Answer: Yes and no! Politico feminism like postmodern feminism recognizes that gender roles are socially constructed. Women and men are expected to behave differently and these roles are a social construction. In fact, politico feminism goes one step beyond and explains the historical account of gender construction. However, politico feminism is different in the aspect that it emphasizes collectivism. Nothing may be permanent in our identity, but it does not mean issues that we face are different. Of course, intersections such as race, ethnicity, class, nationality, and sexuality may be factors, but politico feminism incorporates them in its strategy and policies.

Question 24: Is politico feminism going to lead the fourth wave of feminism?

Answer: Of course, It is going to lead the fourth wave of feminism. If you analyze the successes of the first and second waves, you will notice that women struggle as a separate class and they are united in their demands and efforts. However, when you analyze the third wave, you get to know that only awareness of gender inequality has widely proliferated, but it has failed to turn into a mass movement since the third wave refuses sisterhood. Politico feminism recognizes intersections and different experiences of women as its core principle is to bring such women into power corridors so that their issues could be heard and addressed. You may quote Me Too movement, but it died down as quickly as rapidly it rose. The reason being that no collective strategy was in place to act upon. Fourth wave is going to be all about getting the ultimate goal, gender parity.

Question 25: Separate electorate is for advanced nations or developing nations?

Answer: Separate electorates in the first phase are for the advanced nations where women enjoy more rights than those women in developing nations. Movements in developing nations should be initiated, but advanced nations would spearhead the campaign for separate electorates. Politico feminists shall make international alliances and politico feminist parties would open in each and every country of the world with the same or modified party manifesto, keeping in mind intersections and culture. However, two main elements are always going tobe the same in politico feminist manifestos: demand for separate electorates and collectivism. Right to vote, for example, was first achieved in the advanced nations which paved a way for developing nations to follow suit. Similarly, social protection, maternity leaves, legal protection of rights enjoyed by women all around the world were first achieved in advanced nations. Therefore, international politico feminists' organizations and alliances would facilitate the collaboration and success of the movements.

Question 26: How long will it take you to achieve gender equality?

Answer: We cannot give you a definite answer to this question. We can however surely say that gender equality will be achieved since policies of politico feminism would eventually deliver gender parity in society.

Question 27: Tell us any such policy in detail?

Answer: Education policy can be implemented to mold psychology and behavior of the next generation to accept gender equality as reality. Psychoanalytical feminism has already established that language and childhood experiences shape our personality and gender roles. Education is the process of learning and unlearning. By inculcating feminist literature in school colleges and universities, we can create the foundation of an egalitarian society.

Question 28: Politico feminists are a separate party from other feminist?

Answer: No. They are not a separate political party, but they actually represent them. Like all other feminists, they wish to achieve gender equality, but they have a clear vision as to how they can achieve this goal. Politico feminists are distinguished from other feminists: 1. In the national struggle of different feminists of different countries, politico feminists not only point out common interests of all genders, but also bring them to the front independent of nationality. 2. In various stages, they always stress that women, including other entities, need to establish themselves as a separate political identity. Other feminists also want to achieve gender equality, but they consider different causes of gender inequality. Some feminist point out patriarchy and economy, and others single out gender construction. Politico feminism encompasses all of these strands of feminism.

Question 29: Do you have any message for people?
Answer: Oh! Subjugated genders of the world unite in thoughts and actions under the banner of politico feminism. You have nothing to lose and the world to gain, rights to achieve, injustice and discrimination to end, freedom to gain and break the chains of gender roles expectation.

Bibliography and reference page:

- The Captive Bird is the poem written by Forough Farrokhzada. https://allpoetry.com/poem/8542639-The-Captive-by-Forough-Farrokhzad

- Will Durant , "HEROES OF HISTORY: A BRIEF HISTORY OF CIVILZATION FROM ANCIENT TIMES TO THE DAWN OF MODERN AGE", 2001

- Dr. Vidya Dhar Mahajan, POLITICAL THEORY, 2006